D0773622

UTAH

The Beehive State

BY
JOHN HAMILTON

Abdo & Daughters
An imprint of Abdo Publishing | abdopublishing.com

abdopublishing.com

Published by ABDO Publishing, a division of ABDO, PO Box 398166, Minneapolis, Minnesota 55439. Copyright © 2017 by Abdo Consulting Group, Inc. International copyrights reserved in all countries. No part of this book may be reproduced in any form without written permission from the publisher. ABDO & Daughters™ is a trademark and logo of ABDO Publishing.

Printed in the United States of America, North Mankato, Minnesota.
072016
092016

THIS BOOK CONTAINS
RECYCLED MATERIALS

Editor: Sue Hamilton   **Contributing Editor:** Bridget O'Brien
Graphic Design: Sue Hamilton
Cover Art Direction: Candice Keimig   **Cover Photo Selection:** Neil Klinepier
Cover Photo: iStock
Interior Images: Aaron Jack Halls, Adventuredome, Alamy, AP, Brigham Young University, Discover Moab, Dreamstime, Getty, Granger, History in Full Color-Restoration/Colorization, International Olympic Committee, iStock, Jacobolus, John Hamilton, Library of Congress, Mile High Maps, Mountain High Maps, Minden, Mormon Newsroom, National Park Service, National Weather Service/KTVX News 4 Utah, Oklahoma State University, One Mile Up, Photographic Solutions/Allen Macbean, Real Salt Lake, Salt Lake Bees, Salt Lake City International Airport, Tal Sampson, Thomas Hill, U.S. Air Force, U.S. Congress, U.S. Geological Survey, University of Utah, Utah Jazz, Utah State, Utah State Historical Society/Keith Eddington, Washington Secretary of State, Wikimedia, & Yale University Libraries.

Statistics: *State and City Populations*, U.S. Census Bureau, July 1, 2015 estimates; *Land and Water Area*, U.S. Census Bureau, 2010 Census, MAF/TIGER database; *State Temperature Extremes*, NOAA National Climatic Data Center; *Climatology and Average Annual Precipitation*, NOAA National Climatic Data Center, 1980-2015 statewide averages; *State Highest and Lowest Points*, NOAA National Geodetic Survey.

Websites: To learn more about the United States, visit booklinks.abdopublishing.com. These links are routinely monitored and updated to provide the most current information available.

Cataloging-in-Publication Data

Names: Hamilton, John, 1959- author.
Title: Utah / by John Hamilton.
Description: Minneapolis, MN : Abdo Publishing, [2017] | Series: The United
    States of America | Includes index.
Identifiers: LCCN 2015957742 | ISBN 9781680783476 (lib. bdg.) |
    ISBN 9781680774511 (ebook)
Subjects: LCSH: Utah--Juvenile literature.
Classification: DDC 979.2--dc23
LC record available at http://lccn.loc.gov/2015957742

CONTENTS

THE BEEHIVE STATE

Utah is a desert gem set in the American West. It is a land of much variety. There are the soaring, snowcapped mountains of the Wasatch Range, with world-class ski runs. Dense, pine-filled forests and whitewater river rapids contrast sharply with arid wilderness lands and a salty inland sea. Rugged, sun-beaten deserts are so barren it's like being transported to the moon. In the red-rock country of southern Utah, deep canyons and soaring arches litter the landscape.

Utah's first white settlers were Mormon pioneers. Even today, more than half of the state's citizens belong to the Mormon Church, called the Church of Jesus Christ of Latter-day Saints. The church continues to be a big part of life in the state.

As everybody knows, bees are the hardest-working members of the animal kingdom. Utah is nicknamed "The Beehive State" to remind people how hard the early settlers had to work to make Utah the great state it is today.

A lone car drives across Utah's desolate Bonneville Salt Flats.

Corona Arch is a natural sandstone arch near Moab, Utah.

QUICK FACTS

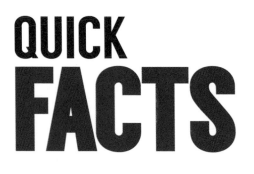

Name: The word *Utah* comes from the Ute Native American tribe, which means "people of the mountains." It may also come from the Apache Native American word *yuttahih*, which means "those that are higher up."

State Capital: Salt Lake City, population 192,672

Date of Statehood: January 4, 1896 (45th state)

Population: 2,995,919 (31st-most populous state)

Area (Total Land and Water): 84,897 square miles (219,882 sq km), 13th-largest state

Largest City: Salt Lake City, population 192,672

Nickname: The Beehive State

Motto: Industry

State Bird: California Seagull

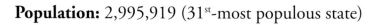

State Flower: Sego Lily

State Rock: Coal

State Tree: Quaking Aspen

State Song: "Utah, This Is The Place"

Highest Point: Kings Peak, 13,528 feet (4,123 m)

Lowest Point: Beaver Dam Wash, 2,350 feet (716 m)

Average July High Temperature: 87°F (31°C)

Record High Temperature: 117°F (47°C), in St. George on July 5, 1985

Average January Low Temperature: 17°F (-8°C)

Record Low Temperature: -50°F (-46°C), in East Portal on January 5, 1913

Average Annual Precipitation: 14 inches (36 cm)

Number of U.S. Senators: 2

Number of U.S. Representatives: 4

U.S. Postal Service Abbreviation: UT

GEOGRAPHY

Utah is located in the American West region. It shares borders with Nevada to the west, Arizona to the south, and Colorado to the east. To the northeast is Wyoming, and to the north is Idaho.

Utah is a "Four Corners State." It shares its southeastern tip with Colorado, New Mexico, and Arizona. Visitors like to come to the Four Corners so they can stand on four states at once.

Most of Utah is called high mountain desert, but there are many kinds of landscapes found in the state. There are rugged mountains, deep river valleys, blisteringly hot deserts, and high plateaus. In the southern part of the state, there are beautiful sandstone spires and arches.

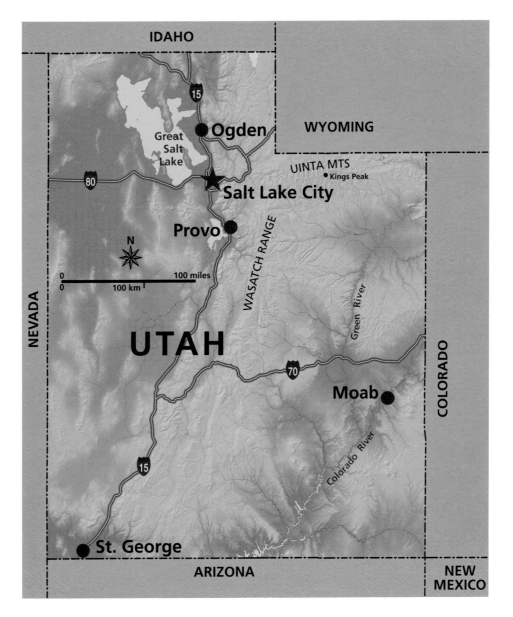

Utah's total land and water area is 84,897 square miles (219,882 sq km). It is the 13th-largest state. The state capital is Salt Lake City.

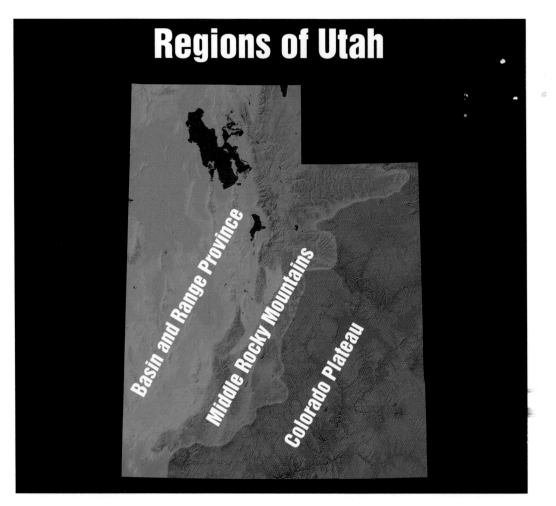

Regions of Utah

Basin and Range Province

Middle Rocky Mountains

Colorado Plateau

Geographers often divide Utah into three main regions: the Colorado Plateau, the Middle Rocky Mountains, and the Basin and Range Province.

The Colorado Plateau is in eastern Utah. It covers about half of the state. There are high plateaus and many canyons. In some places, such as Zion, Arches, and Canyonlands National Parks, wind and water erosion have sculpted strange and beautiful arches and spires into the sandstone rock.

The Wasatch and Uinta Ranges are part of the Middle Rocky Mountains region, which runs through the middle of the state. There are many snowcapped peaks. Utah's highest point is in the northeast. It is Kings Peak, which soars 13,528 feet (4,123 m) high.

The Basin and Range Province is in the west. There are tall, isolated mountain ranges and bowl-shaped valleys. Rivers and rainwater flow into the basins, but the water cannot escape except through evaporation.

The Great Salt Lake is in northwestern Utah. It is the largest lake west of the Mississippi River. It is the remnant of a huge, ancient lake called Lake Bonneville. The Great Salt Lake is 3 to 5 times saltier than seawater. It is very large, covering 1,700 square miles (4,403 sq km) in an average year. It is also shallow, with a maximum depth of just 35 feet (11 m).

There are dozens of rivers and streams in Utah. Through irrigation, early pioneers of the 1800s used rivers to turn parched areas into productive farmland. The two largest waterways are the Colorado and Green Rivers. The Colorado River cuts across the southeastern corner of the state. The Green River is a tributary of the Colorado River. It winds its way southward from the northeastern part of the state and eventually empties into the Colorado River.

Only brine shrimp, brine flies, and some algae live in Utah's Great Salt Lake.

CLIMATE AND
WEATHER

In general, most of Utah is arid. Statewide, it receives about 14 inches (36 cm) of precipitation per year. Parts of the western deserts receive less than 8 inches (20 cm) per year, while some mountain areas see 50 inches (127 cm) or more.

There are four distinct seasons in Utah. Summers are hot, while winters can be extremely cold, especially in the mountain areas. Spring and autumn are usually pleasant, which is why so many people visit the state during those seasons.

A rainstorm at Window Arch in Arches National Park.

People ski through a grove of aspen trees during a Utah snowstorm.

The average high temperature in July is 87°F (31°C). The record high occurred in the city of St. George on July 5, 1985. On that day, the thermometer climbed to a sweltering 117°F (47°C). The average January low temperature statewide is 17°F (-8°C). The record low occurred on January 5, 1913, at East Portal. The temperature that day plummeted to a bone-chilling -50°F (-46°C).

Severe weather sometimes strikes the state, including thunderstorms and blizzards. Because Utah is so dry and mountainous, tornadoes are rare.

CLIMATE AND WEATHER

PLANTS AND
ANIMALS

More than 4,000 kinds of plants grow in Utah. Although the state is known more for its red-rock canyons and flat deserts, forests cover almost one-third of Utah's land area. That is about 15 million acres (6 million ha) of land.

Most of the mountain areas in Utah are forested because there is more water available. There are forests of pine, fir, and blue spruce. Utah's official state tree is the quaking aspen. They are found from upper-elevation slopes down to canyon bottoms. Their leaves turn a brilliant yellow and orange in autumn.

Drought-tolerant trees grow in middle-elevation areas. They include oaks, maples, pinyons, and junipers. Cottonwoods and willows grow near streams.

Utah's Dixie National Forest is filled with aspens, cottonwoods, and pine trees.

Goats graze on desert vegetation in Monument Valley, Utah.

In Utah's large desert areas, the soil is dry and salty. However, many plant species have evolved to grow in these harsh conditions. They include many types of cacti, yucca, sagebrush, and greasewood.

In the mid-1800s, food became scarce in Utah because crickets ate most of the crops. Utah settlers ate the bulbous roots of the beautiful sego lily to get by. That is why today it is Utah's official state flower.

Utah's many different landscapes support more than 600 species of wildlife. Large mammals found living in the forested mountains include elk, bighorn sheep, black bears, and moose. The official state animal is the elk. Only males carry antlers, which may grow to a spread of more than five feet (1.5 m).

Bull Elk

Large animals found all over the state include cougars, mule deer, coyotes, and bobcats. Pronghorn and bison prefer grassland or arid habitats.

Many smaller mammals are found throughout Utah. They include chipmunks, rabbits, beavers, skunks, squirrels, marmots, badgers, prairie dogs, foxes, and many others.

Cougar

Bald Eagle and Gulls

Utah is a wonderful place for birdwatchers. Hundreds of species are found in the state. Some of Utah's larger birds include bald eagles, golden eagles, hawks, many types of owls, and pheasants. Utah's official state bird is the California seagull. In 1848, a horde of crickets devoured crops around the Salt Lake City area. Flocks of gulls appeared and gorged themselves on the crickets, helping save the settlers from starvation. Today, a seagull monument has been built in front of the Salt Lake Assembly Hall in Salt Lake City.

Desert Spiny Lizard

A wide variety of fish can be found swimming in Utah's rivers and reservoirs. They include walleye, northern pike, crappie, whitefish, salmon, largemouth and smallmouth bass, perch, and muskellunge. Cutthroat trout is the official state fish.

Dozens of species of reptiles are found all over the state. They include desert spiny lizards, Gila monsters, painted turtles, and western skinks. More than 30 species of snakes live in Utah. Most are harmless, but seven species are venomous. They include sidewinders, Mojave rattlesnakes, Great Basin rattlesnakes, and western rattlesnakes. Like all snakes, these venomous reptiles are helpful to the state's ecosystems by controlling rodent populations.

PLANTS AND ANIMALS

HISTORY

People have lived in the Utah area for at least 12,000 years, and possibly longer. These nomadic Paleo-Indians were the ancestors of today's Native Americans. They hunted wandering herds of animals with spears and stone spear points. Some lived in small groups in caves or on cliffs.

As time passed, native peoples formed groups, or tribes, and learned how to farm and gather plants. Native American tribes moved in and out of the Utah area through the centuries. Around 1000 AD, several tribes began settling permanently in Utah. They included members of the Shoshone, Ute, Southern Paiute, and Goshute tribes. They were later joined by Navajo Native Americans.

Ute Indians lived on the western slope of the Wasatch Mountains in Utah.

Franciscan friars were among the first Europeans to see the Utah area in 1776.

Among the first Europeans to see the Utah area were Spanish explorers led by Franciscan friars Atanasio Domínguez and Silvestre Escalante in 1776. They were looking for a new route from Santa Fe, in today's New Mexico, to the California coast. Along the way, they sought to convert Native Americans to Christianity.

In the late 1700s and early 1800s, Europeans came and went through the Utah area. Many were trappers in search of beavers. They included mountain men such as Jim Bridger, Miles Goodyear, and Jedediah Smith.

In 1847, the first of many Mormon pioneers arrived in the Utah area. In following years, they came by wagons and pushcarts by the thousands. They found an arid land that was filled with challenges.

Years earlier, Joseph Smith was the leader of the Church of Jesus Christ of Latter-day Saints, also known as the Mormons. By the 1840s, a large group of Mormons had settled in Illinois.

The Mormon religion caused alarm among some Americans because of their odd beliefs. Some Mormons practiced polygamy, in which a man could marry more than one wife. In 1844, an angry mob in Illinois killed Joseph Smith. Church leaders decided to leave Illinois instead of facing more violence. Led by Brigham Young, their new spiritual head, the Mormons loaded their belongings into wagons and headed west.

Brigham Young

The Mormon settlers arrived in Utah's Great Salt Lake area in 1847 and decided to make it their home. "This is the right place," Brigham Young famously said.

In the following years, tens of thousands of settlers followed the Mormon Trail to find a new home in remote Utah. Life was difficult at first. They built homes and churches in new towns. They irrigated their farmlands with water from nearby rivers and streams.

The people of Utah requested statehood in 1849. The United States government rejected the request. There was too much anger over the Mormon's practice of polygamy. Many also thought the church was too involved with Utah's politics.

Utah Territory was formed in 1850. Settlers continued to pour into the area. By the late 1850s, there were at least 150 communities thriving in Utah.

In the 1860s, rich veins of minerals, including gold and silver, were discovered in Utah's mountains. A flood of miners entered the territory. The non-Mormon newcomers added to Utah's diversity.

In 1865, conflict between Mormon pioneers and Native American tribes boiled over. The Indians were angry over the growing tide of settlers taking over their land. A series of conflicts broke out. The Black Hawk War was the most destructive. Chief Black Hawk of the Ute tribe led his people against the Mormon settlers. Many were killed on both sides until U.S. government soldiers arrived in 1872. Most of the Native Americans were eventually forced onto reservations.

In 1869, the first transcontinental railroad was completed at Promontory Summit, near Salt Lake City. Now connected by rail to both coasts, Utah was no longer such an isolated place.

In 1890, Mormon Church leaders banned polygamy. The church also became less involved in government. On January 4, 1896, the U.S. Congress approved Utah's entry into the Union as the 45th state.

A prospector is caught illegally searching for gold on Ute land in the Utah Territory. A flood of miners entered the territory in the 1860s.

On May 10, 1869, Union Pacific and Central Pacific Railroad workers celebrated the completion of the first transcontinental railroad at Promontory Summit, Utah.

After statehood, Utah continued to grow. Farming, railroads, coal mines, and other industries drew people to the state. The Great Depression of the 1930s hit Utah hard. However, during World War II (1939-1945), the state's economy got a much-needed boost. Farmers sold their crops, and several U.S. military bases were built in Utah.

Today, electronics, research centers, and medical facilities have helped Utah prosper. Tourism has become increasingly important to the state. To preserve Utah's natural beauty, both the federal government and the state have set aside millions of acres of parks. The most popular include Zion, Canyonlands, Arches, Bryce Canyon, and Capitol Reef National Parks, as well as Dead Horse Point State Park.

DID YOU KNOW?

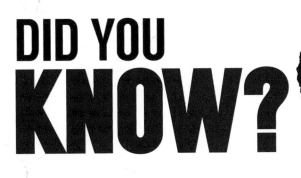

• Millions of years ago, dinosaurs roamed today's Utah. The official state fossil is the *Allosaurus*. This ferocious carnivore grew up to 35 feet (11 m) long and weighed about 4 tons (3.6 metric tons). It had a large jaw filled with sharp, serrated teeth. *Allosaurus* lived during the late Jurassic period. *Stegosaurus* was another common dinosaur in Utah. A plant eater, it had thick, bony plates that stuck up along its back. It was also a Jurassic-age dinosaur. Today, the fossilized bones of these dinosaurs can be found in places such as the Cleveland-Lloyd Dinosaur Quarry near Price, Utah, and at Dinosaur National Monument near Vernal, Utah. There are also many places in Utah where fossilized dinosaur tracks can be seen.

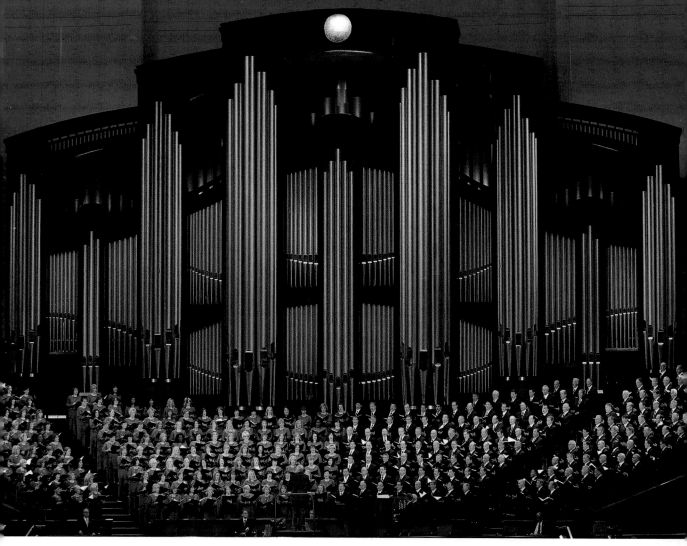

• The Mormon Tabernacle Choir is an amateur choir in Salt Lake City, Utah. It is part of the Church of Jesus Christ of Latter-day Saints. Founded in 1847, the choir today has 360 members. It performs at the Salt Lake Tabernacle in downtown Salt Lake City. (A tabernacle is a meeting place for worship.) The Tabernacle's massive organ has more than 11,000 pipes, making it one of the largest in the world. The choir is acclaimed worldwide for its music, and is enjoyed by people of all faiths. It has won Grammy and Emmy Awards for its performances.

DID YOU KNOW?

PEOPLE

Brigham Young (1801-1877) was the second president of the Church of Jesus Christ of Latter-day Saints, commonly known as the Mormon Church. He was born in Vermont, and became a Mormon in 1835. After Joseph Smith, the church founder, was murdered in Illinois in 1844, Young took a leadership position. He became president of the church in 1847. That year, he led a large group of followers across the country to Utah in order to escape religious violence. Young directed thousands of additional Mormons to come to Utah. Starting in 1851, Young served as the first governor of Utah Territory. His leadership helped Utah's citizens prosper. He continued to lead the Mormon Church until his death at age 76 of a ruptured appendix.

Chief Pocatello (1815-1884) was a war chief who led the Shoshone Native American people during a very difficult time in their history. Pocatello was born in northwestern Utah. In the 1840s and 1850s, large numbers of Mormon pioneers settled on Shoshone land. The newcomers disrupted Utah's ecosystems, causing a loss of wildlife the Indians depended on. Many starved. Many others succumbed to new diseases, such as smallpox, that were brought by the settlers. Chief Pocatello led a series of attacks against the Mormons. Finally, after many battles, he made peace with the settlers. He tried to help his people when they were forced by the United States government to move to reservations in Idaho, far from their ancestral homes in Utah. Today, the city of Pocatello, Idaho, is named in his honor.

Reva Beck Bosone (1895-1983) was the first woman from Utah elected to the United States House of Representatives. Born in American Fork, Utah, she became a lawyer in 1930. She was elected to the Utah State House of Representatives in 1933. She also served as a judge in Salt Lake City before being elected to Congress. During her years in Washington, DC, she focused on helping women, children, and the poor.

Philo Farnsworth (1906-1971) was a television pioneer. He held more than 300 patents for his radio and television inventions. Born in Beaver, Utah, he first came up with the idea for an electronic television system while in high school. In 1927, his experiments resulted in the transmission of the first television image. Farnsworth continued inventing all kinds of electronics during his career, including a device that could detect submarines, and an infrared telescope.

Butch Cassidy (1866-1909) was a cattle rustler and bank robber. Born in Beaver, Utah, his real name was Robert Leroy Parker. Cassidy had a partner named Harry Longabaugh, better known as the Sundance Kid. They led a gang of rustlers and robbers called the Hole-in-the-Wall Gang. After fleeing lawmen in the United States, Cassidy and Longabaugh probably died in a shoot-out in Bolivia, South America, in 1908.

Robert Redford (1937-) is a Hollywood actor and director. He was born in California, but has made his home in Utah for decades. He won an Academy Award in 1981 for directing *Ordinary People*. His most popular films as an actor include *Butch Cassidy and the Sundance Kid*, *The Sting*, and *All the President's Men*. In 1981, he founded the Sundance Institute, which runs the Sundance Film Festival in Park City, Utah, for independent filmmakers.

CITIES

Salt Lake City is the capital and largest city in Utah. Its population is about 192,672. It was founded by a group of Mormon Church pioneers in 1847. They settled in a valley near the Great Salt Lake, nestled in the shadow of the nearby Wasatch Range. Today, Salt Lake City is a center for transportation, government, electronics, and agriculture. After the Winter Olympic Games were held in the city in 2002, Salt Lake City attracted many outdoor lovers and tourists. The University of Utah was founded in 1850. It enrolls more than 31,000 students yearly. There are many museums and performing arts centers in the city. Pioneer Day is a major festival held every July 24 to celebrate the arrival of the state's first Mormon settlers in 1847.

Provo is Utah's third-largest city. Its population is about 115,264. It is located south of Salt Lake City, in the foothills of the Wasatch Range. Originally the home of Ute Native Americans, Mormon pioneers founded Provo in 1849. The city got its name from Étienne Provost, an early French-Canadian trapper in the area. It became known as the "Garden City" because of its many trees, gardens, and orchards. Today, Provo's top employers include education, government, health care, banking, and computer software manufacturers. Brigham Young University, named after the famous Mormon pioneer leader, enrolls about 30,000 students yearly.

CITIES

The city of **Ogden** is located north of Salt Lake City. Its population is about 85,444. Ogden was originally established in 1846 as a settlement and trading post called Fort Buenaventura. Mormon leaders bought the settlement in 1847. It was later renamed Ogden, in honor of Peter Ogden, a fur trapper in the area. Early in the city's history, it became an important railroad hub. The nation's first transcontinental railroad was finished nearby in 1869. Today, Ogden remains a transportation center. Many manufactured goods and farm products pass through the city by train, truck, or airplane. Ogden is also home to Weber State University, which enrolls about 27,000 students yearly. The Ogden Nature Center preserves 152 acres (62 ha) of land that is filled with wildlife exhibits, walking trails, and gardens.

The city of **St. George** is located in the southwestern corner of Utah, near the Arizona border. Its population is about 80,202. Founded in 1861, it was named after Mormon leader George Smith. It is a fast-growing city, thanks to its warm climate, healthy businesses, and easy access to many of southern Utah's national parks. Zion National Park is just 41 miles (66 km) from St. George.

Moab is in the east-central part of Utah, near the banks of the Colorado River. Its population is about 5,235. First settled in 1878 as a farming community, the population boomed in the 20th century with the discovery of uranium, potash, and oil. Today, tourists use the town as a base for hiking, rafting, rock climbing, and mountain biking expeditions. Moab is very close to Arches and Canyonlands National Parks.

TRANSPORTATION

Utah has 46,254 miles (74,439 km) of public roadways. Interstate I-15 runs north and south through the state. It passes through Utah's most-populated cities, including Salt Lake City. Interstate I-80 generally runs east and west. It starts at the Wyoming border in northeastern Utah. It passes through Salt Lake City and then heads west, through the Great Salt Desert, before exiting at the Nevada border. Interstate I-70 crosses south-central Utah. It enters the state at the Colorado border, passes through the San Rafael Desert, and links up with I-15.

Utah's busiest airport is Salt Lake City International Airport.

Seven freight railroads operate in Utah on 1,343 miles (2,161 km) of track. The most common product hauled by rail is coal, followed by chemicals, ores, and farm products. Amtrak's California Zephyr passenger line generally runs east and west through the state. It has stops in Green River, Helper, Provo, and Salt Lake City.

There are about 150 airports in Utah, including small private airfields and military bases. The state's busiest airport is Salt Lake City International Airport. It serves an average of about 22 million passengers each year.

NATURAL
RESOURCES

About 68 percent of the value of Utah's agriculture comes from livestock. That includes beef and dairy cattle, sheep, hogs, and poultry.

Much of Utah is too arid or rocky for farming. To successfully raise crops, many farmers must rely on irrigation from rivers. There are about 18,100 farms and ranches in Utah. They cover roughly 11 million acres (4.5 million ha) of land. That is about 21 percent of Utah's total land area.

The most valuable crops raised in Utah include hay, wheat, corn for feeding livestock, barley, safflower, and oats. Apples, cherries, and peaches are also grown in the state.

A farmer leads a flock of sheep from grazing lands in Mantua, Utah.

The Bingham Canyon Mine is one of the largest open-pit mines in the world.

Gold, silver, copper, lead, molybdenum, beryllium, zinc, and uranium all come from Utah's vast geologic resources. The state is also a major producer of coal, petroleum, and natural gas.

The Bingham Canyon Mine is one of the largest copper mines in the world. Located southwest of Salt Lake City, it is an open-pit mine that has been in production since 1906. The pit measures 2.75 miles (4.4 km) across and .75 mile (1.2 km) deep. It has produced more copper than any mine in history.

NATURAL RESOURCES

INDUSTRY

Utah's factories produce many kinds of goods, including machinery, fabricated metal products, transportation equipment, food products, chemicals, printing, and even rocket engines. Many high-tech manufacturing companies have recently come to the state, making all kinds of electronic equipment, computers, and computer software. S&S Worldwide, in Logan, Utah, is a leading maker of roller coasters and other thrill rides.

About 61 percent of working people in Utah are employed in the service industry. Instead of making products, companies in the service industry sell services to other businesses and consumers. It includes businesses such as banking, financial services, health care, insurance, restaurants, and tourism.

Utah's S&S Worldwide is a leading maker of roller coasters, such as El Loco, at Adventuredome in Las Vegas, Nevada.

An F-35A Lightning II aircraft flies past the control tower at Hill Air Force Base. Hill AFB is the sixth-largest employer in Utah.

About 16 percent of people in Utah work for the state or federal government. There are several large United States military bases in the state that employ many civilians. Much of Utah's land is owned by the federal government, including parks and national forests. Workers are needed to oversee and maintain these important resources.

Tourism is a huge industry in Utah. People enjoy sightseeing, hunting, skiing, or hiking in the state's many parks. Visitors spend about $8 billion in the state each year, enough to support more than 137,000 jobs.

INDUSTRY

SPORTS

The Utah Jazz is a professional major league basketball team that plays in the National Basketball Association (NBA). The team has won several Northwest Division and Western Conference titles.

Real Salt Lake is a Major League Soccer (MLS) team. In 2009, it won the MLS Cup championship. The Salt Lake Bees are a Minor League Baseball (MiLB) team that plays in the Pacific Coast League.

College sports are very popular in the state. Top-level football teams include the University of Utah Utes, the Utah State Aggies, and the Brigham Young University Cougars.

Utah hosted the Winter Olympic Games in 2002. Today, the state has several world-class ski resorts, including Alta, Deer Valley, Park City, Snowbird, and Sundance.

Millions of people visit Utah each year to whitewater raft, rock climb, or mountain bike. Many people enjoy hiking in Utah's five national parks. One of the most popular is Arches National Park. It contains more than 2,000 natural sandstone arches carved by wind and water over many centuries. There are dozens of hiking trails, including a 3-mile (4.8-km) trek to Delicate Arch, the landmark that appears on the Utah license plate.

A hiker stands under Delicate Arch.

ENTERTAINMENT

Hot air balloons float over Park City, Utah.

The people of Utah love festivals. There are festivals for pumpkins, chili, trees, and even hot air balloons. The Ogden Valley Balloon & Artist Festival features hot air balloons floating over the gorgeous Ogden Valley. The Great Salt Lake Bird Festival has workshops, displays, and tours to birdwatching areas.

Salt Lake City has many performing arts groups, including the acclaimed 360-member Mormon Tabernacle Choir. The Utah Symphony was founded in 1940. Its 85 full-time musicians tour all over the world. Ballet West performs such popular ballets as *The Nutcracker*, *Sleeping Beauty*, and *The Little Mermaid*.

The Pioneer Memorial Museum, in Salt Lake City, contains one of the world's largest collections of pioneer artifacts from the 1800s, including quilts, guns, paintings, and a Conestoga wagon. The Golden Spike National Historic Site celebrates the completion of the first transcontinental railroad at Promontory Summit. There are regular reenactments of the Golden Spike ceremony that officially completed the building of the track.

The Sundance Film Festival is an annual gathering of filmmakers. Held in Park City, Utah, it is a chance for new and independent films to get noticed by Hollywood.

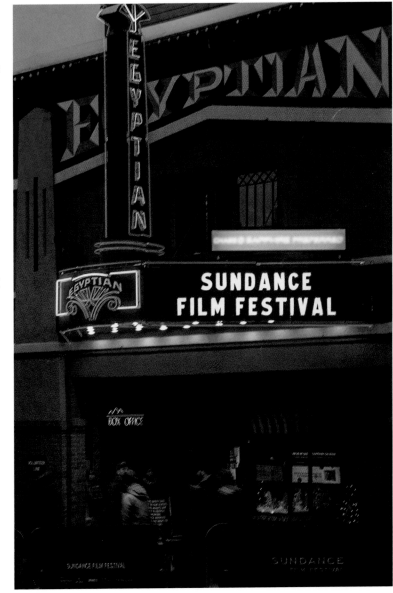

Many of the Sundance Film Festival's movies are shown at the famous Egyptian Theatre in Park City, Utah.

TIMELINE

10,000 BC—The first Paleo-Indians settle in today's Utah area.

1000 AD—Native Americans settle in the Utah area, including members of the Ute, Southern Paiute, Goshute, and Shoshone tribes.

1776—The Domínguez-Escalante Expedition seeks a new route from present-day New Mexico to California. On their way, they explore Utah.

1826—Fur trader and explorer Jedediah Smith leads an expedition to California. The group travels through Utah.

1847—Under the leadership of Brigham Young, members of the Mormon Church arrive in the Great Salt Lake area.

1850—The United States Congress creates Utah Territory.

1865-1868—The Black Hawk War is the last major Native American conflict in the state.

1869—The first transcontinental railroad is completed, with the final spike pounded in Utah at Promontory Summit, northwest of Salt Lake City.

 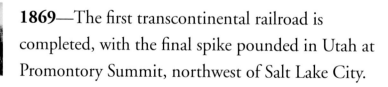

1896—Utah becomes the 45th state in the Union.

1914—Auto racing begins at Bonneville Salt Flats.

1919—Zion National Park is established. It is the first of Utah's five national parks. It is later joined by Arches, Bryce Canyon, Canyonlands, and Capitol Reef National Parks.

1982—The world's first permanent artificial heart, developed by Dr. Robert Jarvik, is implanted into patient Barney Clark's chest at the University of Utah Medical Center.

1991—The Utah/US Film Festival changes its name to the Sundance Film Festival. Based out of Park City, Utah, it becomes the premiere showcase for independent films.

1999—A rare tornado rips through downtown Salt Lake City, causing one death and about $170 million in damage.

2002—The Winter Olympic Games are held in Salt Lake City.

2016—The Environmental Protection Agency (EPA) orders two coal-fired power plants in central Utah to bring their emissions to current standards. Nitrogen oxide pollution from the power plants increases haze throughout the region, including many national parks, creating a health hazard and threatening Utah's tourism.

GLOSSARY

BERYLLIUM

A somewhat rare, gray metal that is both lightweight and strong. It is often used in combination with other metals, such as copper, to create a stronger material.

BLACK HAWK WAR

Beginning in 1865, the Ute tribe led by Black Hawk, a war chief, waged a series of battles against white settlers. It was the last major Indian conflict in the state.

CHURCH OF JESUS CHRIST OF LATTER-DAY SAINTS

Also known as the LDS Church, or the Mormon Church. The first Mormons followed the teachings of prophet Joseph Smith in the early 1800s. Brigham Young became the leader of the Mormons after Smith was murdered in 1844. Young led his followers to Utah to escape further religious violence. The LDS Church headquarters is in Salt Lake City, Utah.

CONESTOGA WAGON

A covered wagon used by pioneers in the 1800s. Drawn by horses or oxen, its floor was curved upward to keep up to six tons (5.4 metric tons) of cargo from shifting while in motion.

ECOSYSTEM

A biological community of animals, plants, and bacteria who live together in the same physical or chemical environment.

Great Depression

A time in American history, beginning in 1929 and lasting for several years, when many businesses failed and millions of people lost their jobs and homes.

Plateau

A large area of land that is mainly flat but much higher than the land that surrounds it.

Polygamy

The practice of a husband having more than one wife. Some early Mormons practiced polygamy, but it was banned in 1890.

Reservation

Land set aside by the United States federal government for Native Americans.

Transcontinental Railroad

An American railroad line that stretched from the Atlantic Ocean to the Pacific Ocean, across the continent. The railroad being built westward (the Union Pacific Railroad) met the railroad going east (the Central Pacific Railroad) at Promontory Summit, near Salt Lake City.

Tributary

A river or stream that flows into a larger river. For example, the Green River flows into the Colorado River in Utah. That makes the Green River a tributary of the Colorado River.

World War II

A conflict that was fought from 1939 to 1945, involving countries around the world. The United States entered the war after Japan bombed the American naval base at Pearl Harbor, in Oahu, Hawaii, on December 7, 1941.

INDEX